Victorian Children

Bre a Williams

www.heinemann.co.uk/library
Visit our website to find out more information about **Heinemann Library** books.

To order:
☎ Phone 44 (0) 1865 888066
▤ Send a fax to 44 (0) 1865 314091
▤ Visit the Heinemann Bookshop at www.heinemann.co.uk/library to browse our catalogue and order online.

First published in Great Britain by Heinemann Library, Halley Court, Jordan Hill, Oxford OX2 8EJ, part of Harcourt Education.

Heinemann is a registered trademark of Harcourt Education Ltd.

© Harcourt Education Ltd 2003
First published in paperback in 2004
The moral right of the proprietor has been asserted.

Editorial: Lucy Thunder and Helen Cox
Design: Jo Hinton-Malivoire, Richard Parker and
    Tinstar Design Limited (www.tinstar.co.uk)
Picture Research: Rebecca Sodergren
Production: Séverine Ribierre

Originated by Ambassador Litho Ltd
Printed in China by WKT Company Ltd

ISBN 978 0431 14621 8 (hardback)
ISBN 0 431 14621 7
07 06 05 04
10 9 8 7 6 5 4 3 2

ISBN 978 0431 14631 7 (paperback)
ISBN 0 431 14631 4
08 07 06
10 9 8 7 6 5 4 3 2

British Library Cataloguing in Publication Data
Williams, Brenda
    Victorian Children. – (People in the past)
    305.2'3'0941'09034
A full catalogue record for this book is available from the British Library.

Acknowledgements
The publishers would like to thank the following for permission to reproduce photographs:
Barnardo's p. **37**; Billie Love Historical Collection pp. **8**, **35**; Bridgeman Art Archive pp. **4**, **9**; Format p. **43**; Hulton Getty pp. **29**; Mary Evans Picture Library pp. **5**, **6**, **7**, **11**, **12**, **14**, **17**, **19**, **20**, **21**, **22**, **25**, **26**, **28**, **30**, **31**, **38**, **40**, **41**; Popperfoto p. **23**; Ragged School Museum p. **16**; Sulham House Collection p. **32**.

Cover photograph of children playing outside reproduced with permission of Topham Picturepoint.

The publishers would like to thank Rebecca Vickers for her assistance with the preparation of this book.

Every effort has been made to contact copyright holders of any material reproduced in this book. Any omissions will be rectified in subsequent printings if notice is given to the publishers.

Contents

Words appearing in the text in bold, **like this**, are explained in the Glossary.

The Victorian age

The Victorian age is named after Queen Victoria. She became Britain's queen in 1837 and reigned until her death in 1901. During her long reign, Britain became the richest and most powerful nation in the world. The **British Empire** included a quarter of the world's land and people.

A changing world

Britain's population grew very fast in the 19th century, from 15 million people in 1801 to over 37 million by 1901. There were many more children than ever before. The average family in 1870 had five or six children. Many Victorian children were born in towns, as families moved from the country to live and work in city factories. Children went to work in the factories, too.

Children born at the start of the 19th century entered a world where nothing went more quickly than a galloping horse. There was no electric power. During Victoria's long life, however, amazing new inventions came thick and fast. In the 1830s, children could wave at puffing steam trains on the railways. By the 1860s, they rode bicycles, watched airships, ate tinned food, and talked excitedly of the latest huge iron steamship. In the 1880s, lucky children could speak on the newly invented telephone, and in the 1890s the first motor cars appeared in Britain.

Victorian children were the first to see the steam railways that carried people and goods from one busy town to the next. This picture is from 1899.

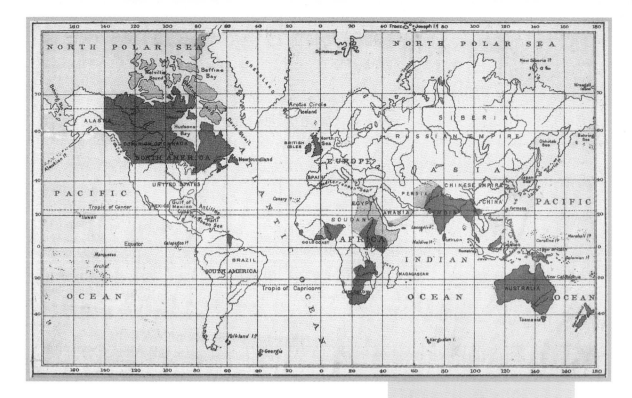

Children of a new age

These changes came about through the **Industrial Revolution**, with its new machines and factories. Many factories employed children, who worked for their living just like adults. They had to make their own way in the world, and that way was often hard.

Victorian children were taught to be proud of the British Empire that was ruled by Queen Victoria. The countries of the empire are shown on this map in red.

In this book, you will learn how Victorian children grew up, about the clothes they wore, the schools they went to and the fun they had when they were not working. Next time you see a Victorian family photo, you will know more about the people whose faces stare at you from the picture frame – and who lived not so very long before us.

Victorian money

The Victorians counted their money in pounds (£), shillings (s) and pennies (d). There were 20 shillings in 1 pound and 12 pennies in 1 shilling. In 1900, a working family of five could spend less than £1 a week. Shops sold lots of things (such as sweets, buns and small toys) for just a penny.

Rich and poor children

The kind of life a child had in Victorian times depended on its family. Were they very rich (**upper class**), fairly rich (**middle class**) or poor (**working class**)? In Victorian Britain, people knew which class they had been born into, and expected to stay there.

Life at the bottom

Children in working-class families had few luxuries, because often their parents were very poor. Their families owned little and paid rent for cramped rooms, damp cottages or small brick houses that were little better than **slums**. Many poor children wore second-hand clothes and went to work, not to school. They were often hungry, and many ran barefoot because their parents had no money to buy shoes. The very poorest children lived rough, sleeping in doorways or sheds. Such children had been abandoned by their parents, or left as **orphans** if their parents had died.

Many poor children in towns were dirty and wore 'hand-me-down' clothes. Some were homeless, sleeping wherever they could find a dry corner, and they either begged or did odd jobs to earn pennies for food.

In the middle

Not all working-class children were poor. Nor were all children in middle-class families rich. Middle-class families included teachers, shopkeepers, farmers, **craftworkers** and office workers. A middle-class child might live in a house with a garden and a maidservant. Middle-class children usually had plenty to eat, wore clean clothes and went to school. They had toys and treats at Christmas and seaside holidays in summer.

At the top

The upper classes included the aristocracy (people with titles such as Lord and Lady) and factory-owners. They were often very rich and could afford big houses with more than one servant. Rich children were usually well fed, clean and well clothed. Boys often went away to school. They had holidays, expensive toys and pets, such as ponies. A Lancashire mill-owner might earn £10,000 a year, while a maidservant in his household was paid less than £30 a year. Their families lived in different worlds.

Moving up

Many poor children, however, started off with hopes of bettering themselves, through hard work or good luck. The Victorians were great believers in what the writer Samuel Smiles called 'self-help'. This meant working hard to improve their social conditions.

This picture shows children enjoying the comforts of a middle-class home. In such homes, boys and girls were clean, warm and well fed.

Who made the world?

The Reverend Francis Kilvert wrote a diary about his life as a country **parson** in the 1870s. When he asked a poor child in his Wiltshire village 'Who made the world?', the child replied 'Mr Ashe'. Mr Ashe was the local **squire**. To that poor child, Mr Ashe – the rich landowner – was as important as God.

The Victorian view of childhood

The Victorians thought family life was very important. It was their belief that the family – parents and children – was the rock on which society stood. In fact, because of the changes made by the **Industrial Revolution**, family life was also being changed. Many people left the villages in which their parents and grandparents had always lived to find work in the city factories. As people moved away, family ties were broken.

The ideal of childhood

Many Victorians had an ideal view of childhood. In a world run by new machines, children's playfulness seemed a reminder of simpler, happier times. People liked paintings of happy, healthy children to hang on their walls. **Advertisers** found that cheerful children on posters or labels helped to sell all sorts of things – from medicine and soap to biscuits and jam.

Like the McCrindle family, shown here in 1894, most Victorian families were large. Few parents, however, were fortunate enough to have all their children survive to adulthood.

Victorians enjoyed pictures that showed a 'rosy' view of childhood, like this one. In reality, however, families knew the sorrows and dangers of bringing up children.

A darker side

When the first photographs of children were taken, in the 1840s, some showed ragged children who lived on the streets. The Victorian ideal of happy, smiling children masked a darker reality. Many children died as babies or youngsters, from one of the many diseases that could not be cured. Others were beaten by cruel parents, employers or teachers, or bullied in tough schools. Far too many children had no families at all. Starving and homeless, they lived on the streets.

Children whose parents died, or children who ran away from home, were all alone. They were called **orphans**, and by law they were put in children's homes called orphanages. These were paid for by local **charities**, but some charities spent little on food or comforts. Charles Dickens told the story of the orphan boy Oliver in his book *Oliver Twist*. When Oliver asks for a second helping of **gruel**, the 'guardians' of his children's home are outraged! (See page 37.)

Funeral children

Many parents had children who died young, so **funerals** were a common part of everyday life in Victorian times. 'Angelic-looking' orphans were hired to take part in them. They walked in front of the funeral procession, looking sweet and sad.

Babies, babies

When a man and woman married in Victorian times, they expected to have children. It was quite common for a first baby to be born within a year of the wedding. The mother might then have a child every year or two for the next fifteen years. Queen Victoria had nine children between 1840 and 1857.

Dangers of childbirth

A Victorian birth could be dangerous, for both mother and child. Women had their babies at home, with the help of a **midwife**. There were no painkillers, until doctors tried out the first anaesthetics in the 1840s. **Hygiene** was poor, too. Many mothers died of fever picked up from midwives (or doctors), who went from one birth to another without washing. One out of every six babies died at birth. Some were too weak to survive; others died because the birth went wrong.

New mouths to feed

Each new baby was another mouth to feed. This could be a burden in poor families, but each new arrival was usually welcomed. The baby was given a gift, such as a pair of tiny knitted slippers. Many babies were taken to church to be christened (baptized). For the ceremony, some mothers dressed the baby in a christening robe, handed down in the family.

The baby carriage boom

Baby carriages or perambulators (Victorians liked long names for things!) were first used widely in Britain in the early 1800s. The early prams were made of wood, with four iron cart-type wheels. There were three-wheelers, too, like some modern buggies. By the 1870s, over twelve firms were busy making baby carriages, either of **plywood** or metal.

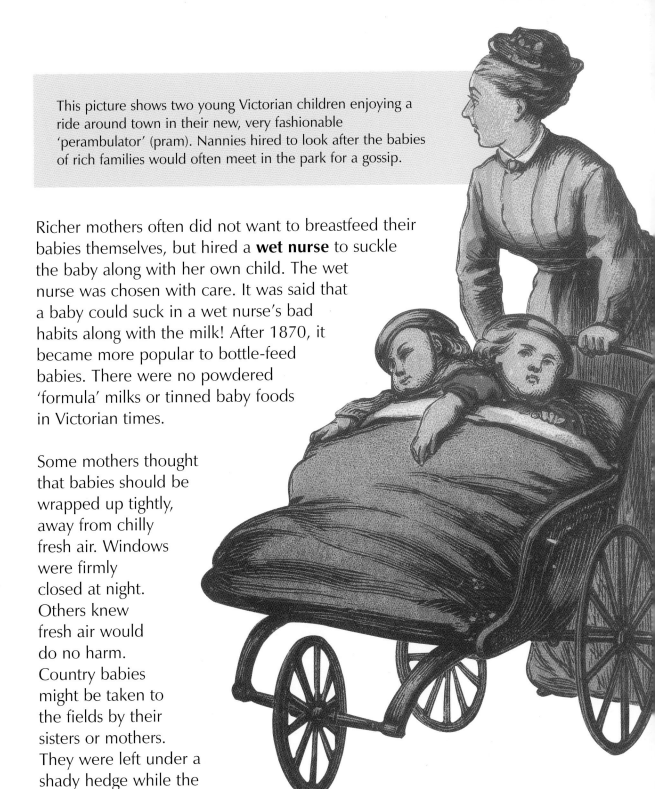

This picture shows two young Victorian children enjoying a ride around town in their new, very fashionable 'perambulator' (pram). Nannies hired to look after the babies of rich families would often meet in the park for a gossip.

Richer mothers often did not want to breastfeed their babies themselves, but hired a **wet nurse** to suckle the baby along with her own child. The wet nurse was chosen with care. It was said that a baby could suck in a wet nurse's bad habits along with the milk! After 1870, it became more popular to bottle-feed babies. There were no powdered 'formula' milks or tinned baby foods in Victorian times.

Some mothers thought that babies should be wrapped up tightly, away from chilly fresh air. Windows were firmly closed at night. Others knew fresh air would do no harm. Country babies might be taken to the fields by their sisters or mothers. They were left under a shady hedge while the family collected leftover wheat or barley stalks.

Growing up

Men had the biggest say in their children's upbringing, although women did most of the caring. Husband and wife were equal partners in some marriages, but it was the man who made the rules in most families.

Spending the day at home

In poorer families, men and women were usually at work all day. So were their older children. The little ones were left at home in the care of a grandmother or neighbour. In richer homes, it was the father only who was usually out working all day. Children too young for school might spend the day in their special room, the nursery. They were looked after by their mother or by a paid **nanny**.

Older children helped to bring up younger ones, especially in poorer families. Most girls learned about babies while helping their mother with the latest member of the family. Young girls were often left in charge of even younger brothers or sisters while their mother was out at work. Children in many homes had to help around the house. They carried coal, peeled potatoes and helped on wash day.

These young boys are wearing skirts. It was quite usual for little boys to be dressed in this way, sometimes until they were five years old.

Nanny, friend and playmate

Richer parents hired a nanny to look after young children before they were old enough for school. The nanny usually lived as one of the family. Winston Churchill (1874–1965) was a future British prime minister. As a boy, he was very fond of his nanny, Mrs Everest, whom he nicknamed 'Woomany'. She, not his busy parents, took him on summer seaside holidays with his brother Jack. Winston Churchill kept in touch with her until her death in 1895.

Coughs and sneezes

Mothers knew that a sneeze might become a cough, and that a cough, could turn into something much worse, such as the disease called tuberculosis. Without modern **vaccinations** and medicines, childhood illnesses, like measles or scarlet fever, could kill. Many children died because infection spread quickly through families. In 1856, Dr Tait, later Archbishop of Canterbury, lost five of his seven children in one month from scarlet fever.

A mother's care could also be harmful. Some women gave fretful babies spoonfuls of gin (an alcoholic drink) or laudanum (a drug) to make them sleepy. Neither 'medicine' was very good for the child.

Safe and sound

Lucky children had safe and happy upbringings. 'There was always the light under the door' one child wrote later, remembering nights in her nursery with a watchful nanny close by. Middle-class children had parks and gardens to run about in, and enjoyed seaside holidays in summer. Poorer children were more likely to be thin and weedy, because they did not have enough good food, fresh air or healthy exercise. A **Sunday school** outing was the only holiday many poor Victorian children had.

Seen but not heard?

Victorian parents often had strict ideas about good and bad behaviour. Punishments ranged from going without supper to being beaten. Pictures on the bedroom wall often showed angelic-looking children. Many stories told of naughty children coming to bad ends. So did the pictures on popular Snakes and Ladders game boards. Smiling, good children were rewarded on the ladders; naughty children had to slide down the snakes!

Many Victorian children went to church or to Sunday school on Sundays. Best behaviour was expected on occasions like this.

Obeying the rules

Victorians loved children, but believed they should learn to behave properly by being given rules, punishments and lessons in good manners. Children were expected to be seen but not heard. At mealtimes, many children were told to eat in silence, except for saying 'please' and 'thank you'. Each child was given a plate of food (no picking or choosing). Many families said grace (a short prayer of thanks to God) before the meal.

Taking what comes

Many Victorian children expected punishment to mean a beating. Some poor children did not know much about religion – or anything else except work. Tom, the little chimney sweep in Charles Kingsley's book *The Water-Babies*, written in 1863, had 'never been taught to say his prayers'. 'As for chimney sweeping, and being hungry, and being beaten, he took all that for the way of the world, like the rain and snow and thunder, and stood manfully with his back to it till it was over…'

Father, mother or a nanny might hand out punishments. They included a severe talking-to, a smack, being sent to bed without supper, missing treats, a dose of nasty medicine or even a beating with a cane. Children in trouble with the police often went to prison. In 1856 there were 14,000 children under the age of sixteen in English prisons. For stealing some tobacco and a bottle of ginger beer, two Portsmouth boys aged thirteen and fifteen were whipped and then jailed for 12 months. This was not unusual.

Prayers for the needy

In religious homes – which usually meant Christian homes in Victorian Britain – children were taught to say their prayers at night before going to bed. They prayed for people less fortunate than themselves. Many children were taken to church or chapel every Sunday or went to **Sunday school**. Many homes had a Bible, which was often read aloud. Not every child was godly, though. In the 1860s, the man who founded the **Salvation Army**, William Booth, was shocked to discover that many children living in industrial **slums** did not even know who Jesus was.

Going to school

At the start of the Victorian age, few poor children went to school, although some were taught by the local **parson.** Many rich boys were sent away from home to live at boarding schools. So were some girls. Most other girls from rich families had lessons at home.

Lessons at home and at work

When wealthy children reached the age of five or six, they might have lessons at home with a male tutor or a female **governess.** Parents who could afford just a penny or two a week sent their children to 'dame schools', run by women childminders or old men. Some **tradesmen** taught the poorest boys in their workshops. John Pounds, a shoemaker, started the Ragged Schools for homeless boys in 1820. These were schools providing free education for poor children who might not otherwise be taught. Many poor children had some instruction in this way. From 1846, older pupils known as monitors were paid a shilling (5p) a week to teach younger children in some schoolrooms.

This picture shows a typical Ragged School classroom. It is in the Ragged School Museum in London.

In his novel *Nicholas Nickleby*, Charles Dickens wrote about a 'horror-school' called Dotheboys Hall where boys were half-starved and cruelly treated.

Schools for all

The 1870 Education **Act** set up school boards to run schools for children aged five to eleven, though not all youngsters of this age went to school. The 1880 Education Act made sure that all children aged between five and ten went to primary school, but even so, many children aged ten to fourteen still went to school only part-time. Until 1891, parents paid a few pennies a week for each schoolchild. Then a new law made primary schools free for all.

Inside the classroom

Many small schools had one big classroom, in which children sat in rows at wooden desks. Reading, Writing and Arithmetic were the main lessons, with Scripture (the Bible) every morning. Children who misbehaved were made to stand in the corner with their hands on their heads. Bad boys were smacked with a cane.

Some school classes were much bigger than today. In 1870, class sizes were set at 60 to 80, but village schools might have just a few pupils.

Hard at work

Victorian children wrote on slates with slate-pencils. The slate could be rubbed clean, and used again and again. Some pupils had paper and pencils, or pens that they dipped into inkpots. They did sums, and copied alphabet letters or 'improving' sentences such as 'A fool and his money are soon parted' or 'Waste not, want not'.

Going to work

'I had rather work than play', said James Orton, a country boy in Kent in 1843. His reason was that he got more food for working. The Victorians thought people who did not work were 'undeserving'. For many children, though, work was dangerous and exhausting.

Hard and dangerous

In previous ages, most children had worked alongside their parents in the fields. In early Victorian Britain, children still did this, but they also worked in industry as well. Children had jobs in coal mines, **mills** and factories. Many started there at the age of five, and did work that harmed their health. Some jobs could cause serious injuries, or even death, as tiny children crawled beneath dangerous machinery. Others scrambled on hands and knees in cold, dark coal mines.

Some Victorians saw nothing wrong in this. Children who worked hard would 'better themselves'. A best-selling book of 1859 was called *Self-Help*. Its author, Samuel Smiles, told stories of children who had risen from rags to riches, through hard work. Very few child-workers were so fortunate.

Chimney boys and mudlarks

Children's work was often dirty. A chimney boy worked for a chimney sweep. His job was to scramble up inside the chimney, to scrape and brush out the soot. He came down covered in soot, and with bleeding elbows and knees. Some boys got stuck and died of suffocation. A 'mudlark' also got filthy dirty. He (or she) waded about in the stinking mud of the River Thames, looking for anything they could sell, such as scrap metal or lost jewellery.

Putting things right

The **reformer** Lord Shaftesbury persuaded Parliament to pass the first Factory **Act** in 1833. This law fixed the working time for children aged nine to thirteen at no more than 48 hours a week. The Mines Act of 1842 stopped all girls, and boys under ten, from working underground in coal mines. It was a start.

More Factory Acts followed in 1844, 1847 and 1878. In 1870, a government **schools inspector** found that only one-third of children in Leeds, Liverpool, Manchester and Birmingham were in school. The Factory Act of 1878 banned the employment of children under ten years of age, but poor families needed the extra money so many children still skipped school.

By 1899, the school-leaving age was raised to twelve. Older pupils often went 'half-time', spending their last year half at school and half at work, learning a trade.

A chimney sweep with his boys. The boys had to be small enough to climb up inside narrow, twisting chimneys.

Clothes and hair

Older Victorian children dressed like little adults, in clothes made of wool or cotton. Children's clothes were thick and heavy, especially a boy's jackets and trousers, and a girl's **petticoats**. Washing them was hard work. Victorian toddlers, especially the well off, were often dressed in frilly clothes. Mothers dressed both boys and girls in skirts long after they began walking.

Hand-me-downs

Most small children wore 'hand-me-downs', clothes passed on by older brothers or sisters. Only rich families bought new clothes from a dressmaker or one of the new department stores.

By the age of ten, many **middle-class** children wore what look to us like adult work clothes. Small boys wore breeches (knee-length trousers) or short trousers, with long socks. When they were about ten, they went into 'grown-up' suits of long trousers, jackets, waistcoats, shirts with stiff collars, and caps. Almost all Victorians wore hats of some sort when outdoors. Little middle-class girls wore ankle-length **pantaloons** beneath their skirts. Some teenage girls wore **corsets**, to squeeze in their waists.

For school, many girls wore white aprons called 'pinafores' over their dresses, as shown here in this school photograph. They were easier to wash and dry than dresses. Boys wore jackets and shirts with large white collars.

Little sailors, little lords

In 1846 Queen Victoria's oldest son was seen in a sailor suit. Soon many boys from richer families were also running around in their own sailor suits, complete with a round-brimmed hat. The American children's book *Little Lord Fauntleroy* (1886) set a fashion for dressing little rich boys in velvet suits with lace collars. Ragged-trousered street children laughed at their 'sissy' appearance.

Keeping warm

In cold weather, many children wore thick woollen underwear, to keep out chills. Outdoors, small children wore hats held on with elastic, and often a shawl. Sometimes a long scarf was criss-crossed over the chest and tucked into the belt of the coat. Shoes were expensive. Some children wore high-sided boots, but poor children often went barefoot, even in winter.

Hair care

Most boys had their hair cut at home, by their mother. Some mothers put off cutting their sons' baby curls until they went to school. Girls with straight hair had it curled at home, using wire curlers and little screws of paper and ribbon. Many girls were told to brush their long hair 100 times a day, to keep it shiny.

Children's boots had thick nailed soles – just like adults' – for tramping over cobbled streets and stony country lanes. Boots and shoes were handed down and repaired until they fell to bits. Children then had to go barefoot, like some of the poor children seen here.

Food, health and hygiene

A good diet is important for health, but in Victorian Britain few poor children started the day with a good breakfast. Most munched a slice of bread spread thinly with butter, or more often **lard** or **dripping**. Luckier children ate porridge, with a spoonful of dark treacle dripped into it.

In richer families, food was usually plentiful, though the menu seldom changed. Lady Eleanor Acland, writing about her childhood in the 1880s, remembered having boiled eggs for breakfast three days a week, with bread and milk on the other days. Dinner (at midday) would be roast meat and boiled potatoes, followed by milk pudding or stewed fruit. Tea was usually bread and jam, with sponge cake. Lady Eleanor had milk and biscuits for supper.

IF I MUST BE WASHED WASH ME WITH VINOLIA

Cold washes and chilly toilets

Children washed in the **scullery** sink or in a basin kept in the bedroom. Water usually came from the kitchen pump, since few homes had a bathroom or taps. At bath time, children sat in a small metal bath put in front of a coal fire. Not everyone had a toothbrush, and toothpaste in a tube did not appear until the 20th century. Many children cleaned their teeth with water, using their finger or a rag dipped in a cleaning powder.

Soap **advertisers** found that pictures of children helped to sell their products. So did the makers of medicines and 'tonics' for small children. This soap advert is from around 1895.

Few Victorian children ever used an inside flushing toilet. At night, most children made do with a **chamber pot** kept under the bed. The rest of the time, they went outside to the **privy**. Flushing indoor toilets did not become common until the late 1800s. Toilet paper on a roll was not available until 1879.

Childhood diseases

Most Victorian children walked to and from school. This helped to keep them fit. Even fit children, however, sickened and died from diseases such as scarlet fever and diphtheria. Children living in **slums** sometimes suffered from **rickets** (caused by poor diet, which gave them crooked or 'rickety' legs) or tuberculosis (a lung disease then known as 'consumption').

Doctors eventually found **vaccinations** and cures for most of the child-killing diseases. Yet year by year many Victorian children died, despite their parents' love and care.

Medicines

Shops were full of medicine bottles and pills, for every childhood complaint. Many mothers 'dosed' their children regularly with castor oil to keep them well. They also spooned out cough mixtures, 'strengthening tonics', or liquorice powder to stop constipation.

The doctor/scientist Louis Pasteur (1822–95) sitting with some of the children he helped. These children were bitten by dogs and were sent to him for vaccinations against the disease rabies.

Games and sport

Victorian children had a lot of freedom. With no cars, the roads were quieter and safer than today's. Country children roamed through woods and fields pretty much as they liked. In the city **slums**, children were left to make their own amusement: climbing lamp-posts, playing hopscotch, or dancing to the music of a hurdy-gurdy man – a street musician who played a small organ by turning a wheel.

There were no children's playgrounds. Victorian parks were like formal gardens, meant for adults to stroll in, not for children's games. So children played wherever they could, in town or countryside.

Fun and games

Traditional fun included April Fools' Day jokes, such as sending a younger, innocent child to buy 'pigeons' milk'. Groups of children played chasing and tag games, with names such as Bull in the Ring. For a furious hockey-like game called Shinney, they used wooden sticks and a ball (or an old cork from a beer barrel).

Children might stage a Jingling Match, in which one player wore bells on his knees and tried to dodge the others, who were blindfolded. At country fairs, children (and adults) scrambled to catch a pig covered in slippery soap, while in Oxfordshire, girls chased a lamb, which they had to grab with their teeth, and so be named Lady of the Lamb!

Egg Shackling

Some games were played at traditional times. Egg Shackling was one of them. On Shrove Tuesday (Pancake Day), children wrote their names on eggs, which they took to school. The eggs were placed in a sieve that was then shaken. One by one the eggs cracked and broke. After this rather messy business, the owner of the last whole egg won a prize.

The Reverend Francis Kilvert noted in his diary for 17 January 1875 that he had met two small children playing at dusk in a waterlogged 'common field' near his Wiltshire home. One boy was blindfolding his little brother, and told the vicar solemnly that 'we'm gwine to play at blindman's buff'. The brothers only had each other to find and catch, but were quite happy.

Playing the game

Organized team games were first played in boys' schools. The Victorians were keen on sport and drew up the first proper rules for many games, including football, rugby, tennis and cricket. Children were taught that a good sport believed in 'fair play, team spirit, and playing the game'. Poor children often played ball games in the street, until a policeman chased them off.

The Victorians liked team games, such as football and cricket. They thought team games strengthened the character, especially for boys at school. This painting from around 1880 shows a cricketing hero being lifted up by his teammates.

Toys and books

Victorian children had fewer toys than youngsters today. Poor families made their own, such as clothes-peg dolls and paper windmills. Children with a little pocket money saved their pennies to buy marbles, a spinning top or cheap wooden toys from the 'penny stall'.

Molly Hughes, a writer who grew up in London in the 1870s, remembered window-shopping with her brothers. They peered into toyshop windows to look at shiny **clockwork** engines or dolls with porcelain heads and real hair. Such toys were too expensive for her to buy. At home, Molly and her brothers were happy turning an old cardboard box into a pretend shop or a pirate ship.

Older, traditional toys included the nursery rocking horse. Victorians also liked mechanical toys. These were worked by winding a key or even by tiny steam engines which burned real coal and sent off jets of steam.

New toys

Factory-made toys had begun to replace many traditional, handmade playthings, such as wooden animals and rag dolls. Tops and hoops were put aside for new talking dolls which said 'Mama' when squeezed; miniature steam engines; train sets and model boats. Queen Victoria collected dolls, and loved dressing them. In many rich homes, elaborate doll's houses had pride of place, as did toy zoos and Noah's Arks, with coloured wooden animals. Boys were given drums and trumpets, as well as boxes full of lead soldiers to fight battles on the floor.

Shows at home

Victorian children loved dressing up, either at home, or when taking part in organized entertainment. Many acted in outdoor **pageants**, such as those to celebrate the Queen's long reign or the **British Empire**. Toy theatres and puppets were also fun for staging indoor shows. Some rich children were lucky enough to have a toy magic lantern, to enjoy 'slide shows' at home (see page 31).

Stories of 'blood and thunder'

Many books written for Victorian children have become 'classics' that are still read today. Lewis Carroll's *Alice's Adventures in Wonderland* is one. Other familiar titles include Anna Sewell's *Black Beauty*, R M Ballantyne's *Coral Island*, and *Little Women* by the American Louisa May Alcott. Children were eager to read of action and adventure. By the 1870s, *The Boys of England* magazine sold over 250,000 copies a week. It was full of 'wild and wonderful' stories.

Penny dreadfuls

Popular penny magazines, with tales of 'horrible crimes', were known as 'penny dreadfuls'. Some shocked parents threw them away! Instead, they gave their children *The Boy's Own Paper* (which began in 1879). In the 1890s, halfpenny comics such as *Comic Cuts* and the *Halfpenny Marvel* won many readers away from the 'penny dreadfuls'.

Holidays

The main holidays were at Easter, **Whitsun**, May Day, August Wakes weeks (when many northern factories shut down) and Christmas. The Victorians 'invented' the Christmas we know today, with trees, decorations, cards and presents. Before this time, Christmas had been a simple religious holiday.

Christmas time

The first Christmas card appeared in 1843. Most children did not spend their money on cards, but painted their own at home, in between helping their mother to make mincemeat and puddings.

Shops in Victorian times stayed open until late on Christmas Eve. Some families exchanged their Christmas presents on Boxing Day (26 December). On this day, people gave small gifts to their servants and tips (money) to **tradesmen**. After Christmas dinner of turkey or goose, the family would roast chestnuts in the open fire. Even poor families did their best to make a special day of it. For many children, there were home-made presents and simple Christmas treats.

The Victorians pictured Christmas as a warm and glowing family season, full of good cheer. The reality for many poor children was not like this.

Going to the seaside

Some Victorian children travelled by train for their first sight of the sea. They made sandcastles and paddled, rode on donkeys, ate ice cream and watched Punch and Judy shows. The Victorians built many seaside piers. Most children loved to walk along the pier, holding on to their hats in the breeze while watching the waves lap at the supports below. 'Being on the end of the pier, with just sea all round, was like being on a battleship, steaming to adventure', one child remembered.

Special days

May Day (1 May) had its traditions, too. It meant dancing around the **maypole** and parades through the streets. A girl would be chosen as May Queen, to walk in procession and be garlanded with flowers as 'queen for the day'.

Day trips were a real treat, and became popular as the new railways made it possible for many more people to travel. Families took day trips or a week's holiday at the seaside. Children were taken on 'outings' by **Sunday schools**, for picnics in local beauty spots. A few rich children were taken to France or Switzerland by their parents, but most never went abroad.

These London children are making the most of good weather paddling in Archbishop Park, London. Some things never change!

Entertainment

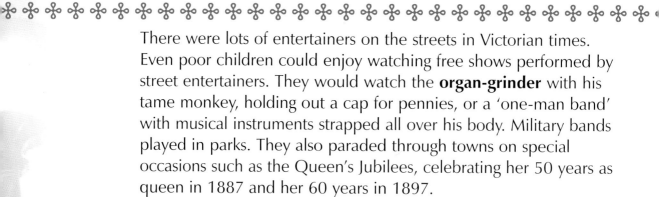

There were lots of entertainers on the streets in Victorian times. Even poor children could enjoy watching free shows performed by street entertainers. They would watch the **organ-grinder** with his tame monkey, holding out a cap for pennies, or a 'one-man band' with musical instruments strapped all over his body. Military bands played in parks. They also paraded through towns on special occasions such as the Queen's Jubilees, celebrating her 50 years as queen in 1887 and her 60 years in 1897.

A trip to the theatre

Theatres and **music halls** were mostly for adults, but older children often got in to watch thrillers with murders, kidnappings, wicked **squires** and sword-fights. The Christmas pantomime was a favourite with rich and poor – poor children were often hired to perform in the chorus as 'crowds' or dancers. Children cheered the heroes (such as Robin Hood or Dick Whittington). They hissed the villains (the Sheriff of Nottingham or King Rat) and laughed at the **Pantomime Dame,** who might be played by a famous male comic actor.

Fairs and circus shows

Another eagerly awaited treat was the arrival of the touring fair or circus. Lots of fairs moved from town to town, with their horse-wagons and steam engines.

This picture shows a family watching a Christmas pantomime. Going to the pantomime became an annual treat for lucky children.

The zoo was another attraction for children. There they could see animals, such as tigers and elephants, from different parts of the world. A ride on an elephant was a thrilling treat. Zoos were known as zoological gardens in Victorian times.

There were rides, stalls and sideshows, in which they could peer at the 'Terrifying Tattooed Man' or 'The World's Longest Snake'. A circus parade took its wagons, caged lions, camels, horses and elephants through town for all to see. Children could get free tickets in return for handing out handbills (advertisements) to passers-by.

Family fun

Many families also entertained themselves at home. There were no televisions in Victorian times, so families played cards, board games or charades. They also played musical instruments, sang and danced. They went for rides in horse-drawn wagons and carriages. Town children enjoyed sitting on top of a horse bus, looking down on the world.

The magic lantern

Magic lantern shows were hugely popular. People watched at home or in a local hall. The lantern was a lamp burning oil or gas, which sent a beam of bright light through a glass lens on to a screen. A picture on a glass slide was slipped into the lantern. It then appeared, larger, on the screen, like a television picture. Lanterns with two or three lenses made it seem as if figures were actually moving – even more exciting!

Country children

⚜ ⚜

Many country children were poor, especially if their parents were farmworkers, whose wages were low. The very poorest children lived in tumbledown shacks, or wandered around the countryside doing seasonal jobs, such as fruit picking in summer. Gypsy children travelled and lived in horse-drawn carts.

On the whole, it was better to be poor in the country than in the town. Country children had fresh air and fields to play in (when they were not working).

Country children, like the three on the right, helped their parents at harvest time. These children are gathering hay into bundles after it has been cut by the adults.

May Day in the country

For May Day, country children picked flowers and greenery, to make a special arch-shaped decoration, which they carried around the village. Inside the garland sat a doll known as the Lady. A girl was chosen to be the May Queen, another to be 'Mother' (who carried sandwiches made by thoughtful mothers) and another was 'Ragman' (who carried coats taken off by tired walkers). Each time the children stopped at a house, they hoped to be given a penny or two. The money was shared out at school the next day.

Gleaning for the family

Farmworkers' children often missed school to help with work on the farm, especially at harvest time. Small children went 'gleaning' with their mothers. They helped collect corn stalks left behind by the harvesters. By nightfall the family would carry home a good load. They gave the grain to the miller, who ground it to flour, which he sent back in a sack. This could be used to make bread, cakes and puddings.

The cottage life

Many country children lived in cottages without piped water. They washed with rainwater that had been collected in a barrel, and went outside to use the **privy**. At night, there were no gaslights, as in the towns. Candles and paraffin lamps gave a soft glow indoors, but on a moonless night all was dark, unless glow-worms were shimmering in the hedgerow.

Wildlife experts

The Victorian countryside was richer in wildlife than it is now. Country children had to watch out for the **gamekeeper**, who guarded his pheasants and trout from **poachers**, and shot 'vermin', such as hawks and stoats. Children knew the names of most wild animals and plants growing around the village. They did not always treat animals kindly – taking birds' eggs from nests, for instance. A few children became junior poachers, 'tickling' trout from a private stream, snaring rabbits or knocking down roosting pheasants from trees with stones.

Townies together

By the end of the 19th century, most Victorian children were 'townies'. Their families had moved to the city to work in the new factories. They often had a harder time than their country cousins and their small houses were usually overcrowded. In large families it was not unusual for some children to eat standing up, or squatting under the table! On bath night, all the children were washed in the same tin bath in the kitchen. Then their clothes were dunked in after them.

Benjamin Seebohm Rowntree belonged to a rich chocolate-making family. In the 1890s, he visited poor families in his home city of York. He was shocked to see whole families living in one room. Parents and small children shared the only bed, while bigger children slept on the floor.

Running wild

Not surprisingly, some poor town children ran wild out of doors. This alarmed their own parents, as well as **middle-class** families in surrounding districts. Many parents welcomed the efforts of **Sunday schools** and new youth organizations to help turn youngsters into good citizens. Among the youth groups were the Band of Hope (started in 1847), which campaigned against alcoholic drink, and the Boys' Brigade (started in 1883).

Off for a day out

One girl in Bristol joined the Band of Hope because her friends went every Tuesday. Many years later she recalled that on her way home from meetings, she fetched her mother a jug of beer from the local shop. It seems the Band of Hope's anti-drink message had not hit home. She liked the outings, though. Everyone piled into wagons. 'We used to pay a penny. Put all the chairs in the furniture van and get in. Go up on the Downs and have a sing-song.'

Marching to the band

William Smith began the Boys' Brigade in Glasgow with 30 members. It grew rapidly. The Brigade was rather like the later Boy Scouts. Its lads wore a soldier's-style uniform, and marched to a brass band. By the 1890s, the Brigade was sending boys on camping holidays.

Boys' clubs were started in some large towns during the 1870s. These clubs were often run by churches, and helped by volunteers from the local boys' school. The best clubs offered boys a warm room, a library with a few books and a game of football, draughts or chess. Poor boys could mix and chat with boys from other backgrounds. Girls were thought less of a 'problem'. Before 1900, town girls had few chances to join clubs or youth groups, but some did.

For town children, joining a youth organization gave them a chance to meet new friends and escape the dangers of street life. Many boys just liked to march up and down, blowing trumpets or flutes and banging drums.

On their own

By the age of twelve, many Victorian children were at work. Like today, most lived at home until they left to find better jobs or get married. However, some boys as young as twelve left home to join the army or navy.

Street children

Thousands of poor children looked after themselves. Many were **orphans**, others were simply neglected. In 1865, the preacher William Booth walked through Victorian London to teach Christianity to the poor. He was shocked to see drunken women feeding beer to their babies, and toddlers picking through stinking rubbish for scraps of food. In the 1850s, as many as 20–30,000 youngsters were living rough in London. To buy bread, they sold matches, firewood, buttons or bootlaces, cleaned shoes, ran errands and swept road crossings. Many boys and girls were sucked into crime, just to feed themselves.

Barnardo's boys

An Irishman named Thomas Barnardo explored London's backstreets at the same time as William Booth. He first came to London in 1866, intending to go to China as a medical **missionary**. Horrified by what he found in the city, he decided to stay and help.

Oliver Twist in darkest London

Charles Dickens wrote *Oliver Twist* in the late 1830s. Oliver first sees London's backstreets with the Artful Dodger. 'A dirtier or more wretched place he had never seen … There were a good many small shops; but the only stock in trade appeared to be heaps of children … crawling in and out of the doors, or screaming from the inside'. Oliver Twist's story has a happy ending. Charles Dickens knew that many Victorian street children's lives did not.

At one of his Bible classes, Doctor Barnardo talked to a thin, hungry-looking boy named Jim Jarvis. Jim told him he had nowhere to sleep, and asked to stay the night in the mission-hall. He told Doctor Barnardo his story, how he had been orphaned at the age of five, then worked on a river barge before running away from the cruel bargeman. He led Doctor Barnardo through the streets, showing him children asleep in haylofts, under old sacks and in doorways. There were probably up to 30,000 such children in London.

Doctor Barnardo opened a home for boys in 1870. It was the first of many. In 1878 William Booth and his wife Catherine founded the **Salvation Army** to help people on their own and in trouble. These and other organizations helped many youngsters escape from unhappy childhoods into more successful adult lives. Both Barnardo's and the Salvation Army are still helping people today.

Doctor Barnardo rescued hundreds of poor children, like these shown here, from a life on the streets of London.

Pioneer children

Children in school learned which parts of the world, coloured red on the map, were part of the **British Empire**. Some among the children went to live and grow up in faraway corners of the empire.

For these families, the ship was taking them to a new country and a life full of new opportunities.

Every year from about 1840, thousands of children sailed from the British Isles in ships leaving from ports such as Liverpool. Some went to America; others went to countries in the British Empire. Between 1840 and 1914, about 19 million people left Britain. Families went with their children. They were sad to leave their homes and relatives, but hoped to find a better life abroad. They set off for 'new' countries such as Australia, Canada, New Zealand and South Africa.

Helping children emigrate

When she was only sixteen years old, Maria Rye arranged for a family servant to go to Australia. She spent the rest of her life helping girls to **emigrate**, raising money and setting up homes for them. In one year (1862), Maria helped 400 women emigrate. She then began arranging for **orphans** to go to Canada, where they would be trained as servants. By 1897, 4000 girls from Britain had gone there.

Sending children abroad

Sending children abroad seemed a good way to improve their lives. Maria Rye raised money in Britain to send girls to Canada. Caroline Chisholm opened a home in Australia to help newly arrived girls settle and find work. Mrs Chisholm believed that women and children would 'civilize' the **colony** more quickly. She helped single mothers with children by arranging for them to travel with married men 'for protection'. She also lent poor families money to pay their passage (fare) to Australia.

The long voyage

Most **emigrant** children travelled the cheapest way – steerage. This meant being crowded with people and luggage on the decks of a steamship for a voyage that might take from two to six weeks. There was little room to play games on the crowded ship, but plenty of sea air! For some it was a thrilling adventure. Others must have been terrified in stormy seas, as the ship rolled, heaved and groaned, making most of the passengers seasick.

Lots to learn on arrival

Children were usually quicker than grown-ups to adapt to their new world. New little Australians got used to hot sun and unusual plants; new Canadians played in deep winter snow. Emigrant children soon learned which strange animals were harmless (Australian kangaroos, Canadian beavers) and which were best avoided (snakes and spiders in Australia, bears and wolves in Canada). Life was hard at first, but most children quickly settled and did well in their new homes.

The royal children

The royal family was often used by teachers, clergy and others as an example of the ideal Victorian family. Queen Victoria herself had a lonely childhood. She was an only child whose father died before she was a year old. Brought up by her mother, she had lessons at home. She became queen in 1837, when she was only eighteen.

When she married her German cousin, Prince Albert, in 1840, Victoria looked forward to a happy family life. Her first baby was born later that year and, in 1841, she gave birth to her first son. He was named Albert Edward, but the family called him 'Bertie'. In all, the queen had five girls and four boys between 1840 and 1857.

Bringing up the family

Like most Victorian wives, the Queen followed the wishes of her husband on how children should be brought up. Prince Albert had firm views on this subject. He was a playful father who enjoyed games of hide and seek in palace corridors. Yet he was also a stern believer in hard work. Both parents were determined that the princes and princesses should not be spoilt.

This painting from 1847 shows Queen Victoria, Prince Albert and some of their children.

The royal children were happiest at Osborne House, the family home on the Isle of Wight. Here their father taught them woodwork, they dug in their vegetable gardens, 'kept house' in a playhouse known as the Swiss Cottage and played soldiers in a miniature fort. The public and the newspapers took little interest in them – very different from today's royal family.

God bless the Prince of Wales

In March 1863, the *Hampshire Chronicle* newspaper reported that local children in the town of Alton celebrated the wedding of 'Bertie', the Prince of Wales. The 'infant schoolchildren' sang a song to the tune of 'God Save the Queen', and were given oranges and cake. The older children joined a march behind the town band, for more songs. The celebrations ended with a bonfire and fireworks.

Growing up and going away

After Prince Albert died in 1861, Queen Victoria stayed in **mourning** for the rest of her life. She worried a good deal about her children, even when they were adults. Her eldest daughter 'Vicky' married a German prince and went to live in Germany. The Queen missed her, and she and Vicky exchanged many letters, like other Victorian mothers and daughters. In one letter the Queen told Vicky what she thought of the prime minister, Mr Gladstone: 'He is really half crazy, half silly and it is better not to provoke [encourage] discussion [with him]'!

Everyone celebrated royal events, such as the Queen's Diamond Jubilee in 1897. Streets, like St James St., London shown here, were decorated for the occasion.

How do we know?

✤ ✤

Words and pictures tell us a lot about Victorian children. From school and factory records, we know that many started to work at a very young age. From **census** records, which began in 1801, we know that most children lived at home with their parents until they were married. Unmarried children stayed on, sometimes to look after ageing parents.

Smile for the camera

Paintings, drawings and photos also take us into the world of the Victorian child. Studio photographers were kept busy, because parents liked to have a **memento** of their children. Children in photos usually look rather serious because they had to sit still. At first, cameras were heavy boxes, with glass plates inside them. After the invention of cheap roll-film cameras in the 1880s, many families took 'snaps' of their children.

Writings about children

With no television, radio, cinema or computers, Victorians had plenty of time for reading. The novels of writers such as Charlotte Brontë (1816–55) and Charles Dickens (1812–70) tell us about children, schools and parents. Books with child characters, such as Thomas Hughes' *Tom Brown's Schooldays*, were very popular.

The Victorians left a huge mass of government reports on the conditions of children. Reports by factory and **school inspectors**, and by 'investigative journalists' (for newspapers), such as Henry Mayhew, opened people's eyes to the plight of many children. In 1897, Mrs Edith Hogg, reporting for the Women's Industrial Council, wrote about London schoolchildren. She found that 'M.B., aged ten, minds a baby for $6\frac{1}{2}$ hours daily and for 13 hours on Saturday, for 6d and food … C.D. turns a mangle for $3\frac{1}{2}$ hours daily and for 10 hours on Saturday for 2d …'.

An 1883 report from the Liverpool Society for the Prevention of Cruelty to Children tells of 'two motherless girls, aged eight and ten ... known to wander the streets nearly all night'. The National Society for the Prevention of Cruelty to Children (NSPCC) grew out of such local groups, formed by people who cared about children in need.

In many museums around Britain, you can see things that relate to Victorian children. These are school books and a slate.

Things to see

There is still a lot of evidence of Victorian Britain today. Some museums have recreated Victorian schoolrooms, factories and houses. There you can see how children lived, look at their toys and even dress up as a Victorian. With all this evidence, you can gain an idea of what life in Victorian Britain was like for the children who could have been your great-great-grandparents!

Timeline

✤ ✤

1833 Factory **Act** bans children under nine from working in textile factories

1837 Victoria becomes queen

1840s Start of mass **emigration** from Britain and Ireland to USA, Australia, Canada and New Zealand

1840 First training school for teachers set up, in London

1842 New law stops children younger than ten working underground in coal mines

1842 Mines Act stops girls, and boys younger than ten, from working underground in coal mines

1844 Factory Act limits children younger than thirteen to working 6½ hours a day

1847 First Ten Hour Act reduces the working day for women and children under 18 to no more than 58 hours a week

1851 The Great Exhibition is held in London

1861 Prince Albert dies

1870s Prams and bottle-feeding become popular with mothers

1870 Education Act sets up school boards to provide schools for five to eleven year olds, for a small charge

1870 First home for homeless boys opened by Doctor Barnardo

1878 Factory and Workshops Act bans employment of children younger than ten years old

1887 Queen Victoria's Golden Jubilee (50 years as queen)

1889 The National Society for the Prevention of Cruelty to Children (NSPCC) is founded. Britain's first law to prevent cruelty to children is passed

1891 New law makes free primary schooling for all children compulsory

1897 Queen Victoria's Diamond Jubilee (60 years as Queen)

1901 Queen Victoria dies. Her eldest son becomes King Edward VII.
Marconi sends first radio signals across the Atlantic Ocean

Sources

Sources (selected)

A Country Camera 1844–1914, Gordon Winter (Penguin, 1973)

The Diary of the Reverend Francis Kilvert 1870–1879 (Pimlico, 1999)

Dickens' London, Peter Ackroyd (Headline, 1987)

Goodbye for the Present; The Story of Two Childhoods
Eleanor Acland (Hodder and Stoughton, 1935)

The Life of the Fields, Richard Jefferies (Chatto and Windus, 1893)

A London Child of the 1870s, M V Hughes (OUP, 1976)

Oxford Illustrated History of Britain, Ed. Kenneth O Morgan (OUP, 1984)

A Social and Economic History of Industrial Britain,
John Robottom (Longman, 1986)

Sports and Games, Brian Jewell (Midas, 1977)

Victorian Things, Asa Briggs (Penguin, 1990)

The Victorian Town Child, Pamela Horn (Sutton Publishing, 1997)

Victorian Village Life, Neil Philip (Albion Press, 1993)

Willingly to School, Mary C Borer (Lutterworth, 1976)

Further reading

Victorian Britain, Andrew Langley (Heinemann, 1994)

Victorian Children, Jane Shuter (Heinemann, 1995)

Victorian Factories, Andrew Langley (Heinemann, 1996)

Also, look on www.heinemannexplore.co.uk for more information
on the Victorians.

Places to Visit

Bethnal Green Museum of Childhood, London

Castle Museum, York (includes reconstructed Victorian street)

Gunnersbury Park Museum, London (has a reconstructed kitchen)

London Museum, Victoria and Albert Museum, London

Museum of Childhood, Edinburgh

Museum of English Rural Life, Reading

New Lanark Visitor Centre, Lanark

North of England Open Air Museum, Beamish, Co. Durham

Shugborough Estate, Stafford (restored estate)

Weald and Downland Museum, near Chichester, West Sussex

Welsh Folk Museum, St Fagans, Cardiff

Glossary

Act law passed by Parliament

advertisers firms using advertisements to sell their products

British Empire countries ruled by Britain or linked to it (from the late 17th century to the mid-20th century)

census population count collecting information about people

chamber pot china bowl used inside as a night-time toilet

charities organizations set up to raise money for good causes such as the poor or homeless

clockwork machinery wound up by a spring and a key

colony territory ruled or settled by people from another country

corset tight garment laced around the stomach, to make the waist smaller

craftworker worker skilled at handwork, such as a furniture-maker

dripping fat and juices from roasted meat, which hardens when cool

emigrate leave your home country to go and live in another land. People who did this were called emigrants.

funeral ceremony that takes place when a person dies

gamekeeper worker who looks after game birds (such as pheasants) kept for shooting

governess woman employed by a family to teach the children

gruel thin porridge made from oatmeal and water

hygiene keeping clean and free from harmful germs

Industrial Revolution great changes in manufacturing and machinery beginning in the 1700s, but mainly taking place in Victorian times

lard fat from a pig

maypole tall pole with long ribbons, for dancing around on May Day

memento object kept as a souvenir, to bring back happy memories

middle class people who are better off and better-educated that the working class, but less rich than the aristocracy

midwife woman who helps mothers during childbirth

mill factory making cotton or woollen goods

missionary person who spreads their religious beliefs, particularly abroad

mourning period of sadness after someone dies

music hall popular stage entertainment with songs, dances and comic turns

nanny person hired to look after children at home

orphan child with no parents

organ-grinder street musician who plays a mechanical organ

pageant show in which people act out scenes from history

pantaloons long underwear, like baggy trousers gathered at the ankles, worn by Victorian girls

Pantomime Dame comical female character in pantomime, usually played by a man

parson another name for a clergyman or vicar

petticoats underskirts worn for warmth and to make skirts stand out

poacher person who kills animals such as deer, pheasants or rabbits on someone else's land

privy outside toilet usually in a shed or small building

reformer person who tries to change the law to improve things

rickets illness, which makes bones grow soft, caused by not having enough Vitamin D

Salvation Army Christian charity organization whose members wear army-style uniforms

slums poor areas of bad housing, lacking clean water

schools inspector government official sent to check how teachers and pupils are getting on in school

scullery small room with a sink, used for washing-up

squire local landowner, an important person in a country community

Sunday schools classes to teach children about Christian belief and worship. Sunday Schools were usually attached to a church and were first set up in 1780.

threepenny bit small coin, worth three Victorian pennies

tradesman shopkeeper, coalman or skilled workman who might call at a house

upper class member of the aristocracy or someone who is rich and powerful – a factory owner, for instance

vaccinations injections of weak doses of a disease to make people immune (safe) from a more dangerous form of the disease

Whitsun Christian festival of Pentecost, the 50th day after Easter

wet nurse nurse hired to feed a baby with her breast milk

working class in Victorian times, people who worked on farms, mines, docks, factories and at home, doing heavy work usually for low wages

Index